Contents

Let's go biking!

Mountain biking is one of the most popular adventure sports of all time. It is also one of the most modern, as it dates back only to the late 1970s.

In 1979 Americans Gary Fisher and Charlie Kelly set up a business which made bikes that people could ride off-road. Since then, people all over the world have bought tough bikes that will take them over forest tracks and mountain trails, along river banks and even through deserts. The mountain bike revolution has touched the lives of millions of people, wherever they live.

Above *Bike shops all round the world sell mountain bikes.*

Amazing FACTS

There are many types of mountain biking: cross-country, free riding, endurance racing, winter downhill and extreme events. The highest race in the world is held in Tibet, with a grandstand view of Mount Everest. Competitors ride as high as 5,500m, where the air is so thin it leaves them gasping. The route of the longest ever mountain bike race ran for 4,345 km from Canada to Mexico through the Rocky Mountains.

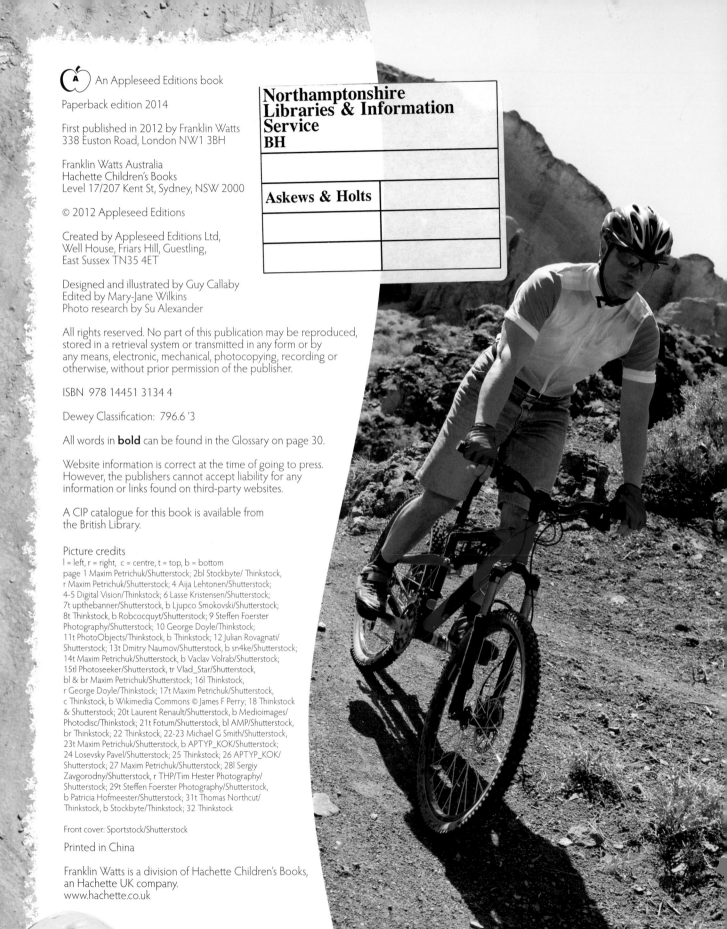

An Appleseed Editions book

Paperback edition 2014

First published in 2012 by Franklin Watts
338 Euston Road, London NW1 3BH

Franklin Watts Australia
Hachette Children's Books
Level 17/207 Kent St, Sydney, NSW 2000

© 2012 Appleseed Editions

Created by Appleseed Editions Ltd,
Well House, Friars Hill, Guestling,
East Sussex TN35 4ET

Designed and illustrated by Guy Callaby
Edited by Mary-Jane Wilkins
Photo research by Su Alexander

ISBN 978 14451 3134 4

Dewey Classification: 796.6 '3

All words in **bold** can be found in the Glossary on page 30.

Website information is correct at the time of going to press. However, the publishers cannot accept liability for any information or links found on third-party websites.

A CIP catalogue for this book is available from the British Library.

Picture credits
l = left, r = right, c = centre, t = top, b = bottom
page 1 Maxim Petrichuk/Shutterstock; 2bl Stockbyte/ Thinkstock, r Maxim Petrichuk/Shutterstock; 4 Aija Lehtonen/Shutterstock; 4-5 Digital Vision/Thinkstock; 6 Lasse Kristensen/Shutterstock; 7t upthebanner/Shutterstock, b Ljupco Smokovski/Shutterstock; 8t Thinkstock, b Robcocquyt/Shutterstock; 9 Steffen Foerster Photography/Shutterstock; 10 George Doyle/Thinkstock; 11t PhotoObjects/Thinkstock, b Thinkstock; 12 Julian Rovagnati/ Shutterstock; 13t Dmitry Naumov/Shutterstock, b sn4ke/Shutterstock; 14t Maxim Petrichuk/Shutterstock, b Vaclav Volrab/Shutterstock; 15tl Photoseeker/Shutterstock, tr Vlad_Star/Shutterstock, bl & br Maxim Petrichuk/Shutterstock; 16l Thinkstock, r George Doyle/Thinkstock; 17t Maxim Petrichuk/Shutterstock, c Thinkstock, b Wikimedia Commons © James F Perry; 18 Thinkstock & Shutterstock; 20t Laurent Renault/Shutterstock, b Medioimages/ Photodisc/Thinkstock; 21t Fotum/Shutterstock, bl AMP/Shutterstock, br Thinkstock; 22 Thinkstock, 22-23 Michael G Smith/Shutterstock; 23t Maxim Petrichuk/Shutterstock, b APTYP_KOK/Shutterstock; 24 Losevsky Pavel/Shutterstock; 25 Thinkstock; 26 APTYP_KOK/ Shutterstock; 27 Maxim Petrichuk/Shutterstock; 28l Sergiy Zavgorodny/Shutterstock, r THP/Tim Hester Photography/ Shutterstock; 29t Steffen Foerster Photography/Shutterstock, b Patricia Hofmeester/Shutterstock; 31t Thomas Northcut/ Thinkstock, b Stockbyte/Thinkstock; 32 Thinkstock

Front cover: Sportstock/Shutterstock

Printed in China

Franklin Watts is a division of Hachette Children's Books, an Hachette UK company.
www.hachette.co.uk

Taking up the challenge

Few things are as exciting as riding a bike down steep bumpy tracks through woods, over riverbeds and deep into the hills. Riders need good bike-handling skills, strength and to be bold enough to take on the challenge. Are you ready to feel the thrill of the ride?

Mountain biking is a sport that can appeal to all the family.

What is mountain biking?

Mountain biking involves riding off-road over rough ground, which is often steep and can be dangerous. The bikes that have been developed since the 1970s to cope with this tough **terrain** have special **frames**, brakes, gears, tyres and **suspension**.

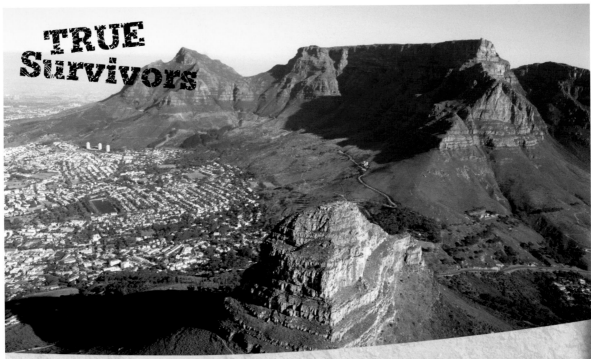

TRUE Survivors

Kenny Belaey is a 28-year-old Belgian mountain biker who has won many competitions and undertaken some amazing stunts. In 2011 he travelled to Cape Town, South Africa, and carried his nine kilo bike to the top of Table Mountain while it was still dark (it is too steep to ride up). He was at the top by sunrise and then performed some amazing stunts at 1,000 metres, including **wheelies** on the edge of cliffs and jumping three-metre gaps (called gapping) over sheer drops. To cap it all, he hopped up on to the cable car wires high above the ground and rode over them. A mistake at any time would have meant a fall to his death.

The bike

Today's bikes are **designed** to cope with the various different styles of riding – including downhill, cross-country, dirt jumping and trial biking. But there are also general mountain bikes that can handle most terrain. They all have strong frames that can withstand bumps and falls, thick tyres to grip dirt, soil, mud or sand, and gears to help riders go uphill on unstable ground. Some also have suspension on the front or rear to help cushion the rider from big jolts and to **absorb** the **impact** of riding over rough ground.

Amazing FACTS

The Cliffs of Moher in County Clare on the west coast of Ireland are more than 200m high, and a top tourist attraction. About a million people a year come to walk the 8 km path that runs between the cliff walls and the sea. In 2010, intrepid mountain bikers Hans Rey and Steve Peat cycled the trail. As they recalled, the trail included a ledge just 10 cm wide and they jumped metre-wide gaps, with hundreds of metres of empty space to fall into if they got it wrong!

Mountain bike trails

There are mountain bike trails in most countries all over the world. They range from simple tracks in towns and cities suitable for all the family, to dangerous mountain descents for experts only. Some have been specially made and others are adapted from ski slopes, dirt tracks or mountain paths.

World's best mountain bike trails

1. **Whistler, British Colombia, Canada** has a 1,200m descent with lots of jumps on the way down. A lift helps riders back up.

2. **Les Gets, French Alps** has two downhill courses and more than 200 km of biking trails.

3. **Cwmcarn, South Wales** has the Twrch Trail, a 15 km long purpose-built mountain bike track, which suits all abilities.

4. **Cancha Carrera, Chile** is one of the best high mountain bike trails in the world – but only for experienced bikers.

5. **Dirt Park, South Island, New Zealand** is an advanced 2 km downhill thrill ride.

6. **Mount Buller, Australia** is a ski resort in winter and given over to mountain bikes the rest of the time. There are four exciting trails to choose from.

7. **Moab, Utah** is one of the best places for mountain biking and suitable for all abilities. The Slickrock bike trail is more than 15 km long and one of the best for advanced riders.

The Yungas Road near La Paz in Bolivia, the most dangerous road in the world.

TRUE Survivors

When Michael Liebreich and Katherine Henderson read about the most dangerous road in the world, they wanted to try it. The Yungas Road (also known as Death Road) is in Bolivia, and runs 69 km from the capital city, La Paz, to Coroico. A vehicle goes over the edge once every two weeks and about 200 people are killed every year. Landslides and rockfalls are regular occurrences and the road is constantly under repair. None of this stops mountain bikers attempting to ride along it, and experiencing its amazing 64 km descent. Michael and Katherine set off in May 2004, only to become involved in trying to save a French cyclist who had fallen over the edge in a moment's loss of concentration, landing 50 metres below. Katherine and Michael learned that you need superior biking skills to travel the Yungas Road and arrive in one piece.

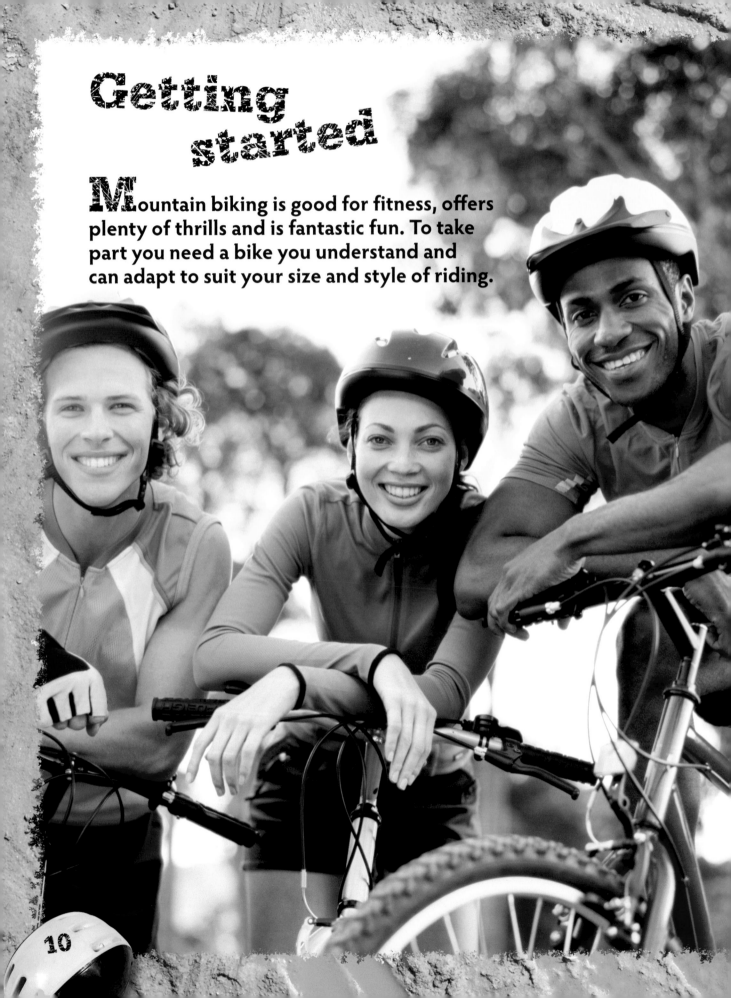

Getting started

Mountain biking is good for fitness, offers plenty of thrills and is fantastic fun. To take part you need a bike you understand and can adapt to suit your size and style of riding.

Joining a club

This is one of the best ways to start and will help you meet other people your age. You might be able to hire a bike and try out the sport before you decide to buy one. Clubs offer expert help from experienced adults, as well as hints and tips from other bikers. You will have an opportunity to learn and develop your skills in a safe environment. Find out whether your school has a mountain bike club. If it doesn't, why not set one up?

Information sources

Organizations such as the scouts and guides offer training in mountain biking. Most countries have national cycling organizations too, offering information and advice on buying your first mountain bike and learning the basic skills. Your local bike shop may have staff who can answer questions and give you hints on how to get started.

Amazing FACTS

Once you've mastered the basics of mountain biking, the sky is the limit. This was true for the young Spanish mountain biker, Bienve Aguado. In January 2011 he made the first ever double front flip on a mountain bike in Barcelona, Spain. He was towed by motorbike towards a dirt ramp more than seven metres high, raced up the ramp and took off at the top. He flipped over twice in mid air and landed on the down-slope on the other side of the dirt ramp.

TRUE Survivors

Competitors taking part in extreme mountain biking can pay a heavy price in terms of injuries. In September 2011, Welsh mountain bike champion Manon Carpenter won the world junior champion title in Switzerland. She had wanted to compete for the title the previous year, aged 17, but had had an accident in the US which resulted in a broken arm. Doctors were able to fit a metal plate, after which Manon rode to success in 2011. Today when Manon competes, she dons body armour, a neck brace and a full-face helmet to protect her from injury when she falls.

Bikes made for mountains

A modern mountain bike is designed to ride over a wide variety of surfaces – including rock, mud, dirt and sand – as well as to go steeply uphill and downhill. It is strong, with powerful brakes, lots of gears, tough knobbly tyres, and even front and rear shock absorbers.

saddle

handlebars

seat post

head tube

top tube

rear brake

front brake

derailleur gear

down tube

spokes

tyre

chain

Made for mountains

Knobbly tyres grip uneven and shifting ground much better than ordinary, flatter road tyres. Some mountain bikers let some air out of their tyres to give them greater stability. This means that on a road, mountain bikes (MTBs for short) are slow – there is lots of **friction** in big tyres. Disc brakes grip the centre of the wheel rather than the rim as on ordinary brakes, which means that they do not become so clogged with dirt. MTBs have between 21 and 27 gears, which allow you to cycle over steep muddy hills provided you are fit. Shock absorbers in the front forks provide stability and also protect your wrists and elbows from the jolting of riding on a hard rocky surface.

Amazing FACTS

The longest mountain bike trail in the world is the Great Divide Trail. It runs from Banff in Canada south across the US through the Rocky Mountains all the way to the Mexican border. It is more than 4,000 km long and a fit cyclist would take about 70 days to travel its length, riding between 40 and 100 km a day.

Banff, Canada

Antelope Wells, New Mexico

WORLD'S STRONGEST BIKE

An American company called Delta & Sports has made an incredibly strong and also see-through bike. The frame is made from carbon fibres mixed with **Kevlar** fibres (very strong synthetic fibres), woven into a tube to make the bike frame. It looks strange, but is stronger than steel or **titanium**. A bike made from this wonder material costs around £8,000!

The right kit

Mountain biking kit should be practical and light to keep you warm in cold weather and cool and dry when it is hot. You should expect to take some falls; they're all part of the fun, but people can be injured.

Clothing

You can wear ordinary clothing: T-shirts, sweatshirts, shorts or trousers and trainers. If you are riding in sunshine, take a sunhat. If the weather is cold and wet, make sure you have a waterproof jacket and fleece. Padded shorts or trousers make longer and harder rides more comfortable.

helmet

windproof jacket

training shoes

A mountain biker kitted out ready to ride.

Above *A full helmet protects your face if you fall.*

Body protection

Helmet All MTB riders wear helmets: they save lives and protect against head injuries and **concussion**. Two thirds of people killed in biking accidents die because of head injuries. Always wear a helmet – on-road or off-road. Modern helmets are light and allow air to reach your head. Downhill racers wear helmets with face guards.

Gloves When you fall, your hands are the first to hit the ground. Gloves prevent cuts and bruises and help absorb the shock of an impact.

Shockproof glasses These protect your eyes from mud and grit thrown up off the trail.

Knee and elbow protectors On tougher trails, these are essential, as knees and elbows usually hit the ground straight after your hands when you fall.

Emergency equipment

If you go on a long trail, take plenty of liquid and food. You can carry it in a **pannier** or on your back in a small rucksack. Also consider taking a mobile phone, bike lights (in case you return after dark), spare clothing, sunscreen and a sunhat, and possibly even a lightweight shelter in case of emergency.

TRUE Survivors

Caernarfon

Cardiff

Forty-one-year-old Welshman Dave Buchanan is a true survivor. In 2011 he set a record for the longest distance travelled by mountain bike in 48 hours with an epic ride across Wales. The ride took him from Cardiff in the south to Caernarfon in the north and back again; 721 km in all. Most of the ride was off-road, and all the ascents put together would add up to 2.5 times the height of Everest. Altogether Dave endured 59 hours of non-stop pedalling in rain and a strong wind – an amazing example of mountain biking grit, determination and survival.

Sizing your bike

Your bike needs to be the right size for you to handle. If it is too big or too small, it will feel awkward and out of balance. An experienced person will help you adjust the handlebars and saddle so they fit you correctly.

Amazing FACTS

When your bike fits you well and you have had plenty of time to practise your skills, there is no telling what you might achieve. The skill is to understand how to handle the bike and where its balance points are. In October 2007, 19-year-old Mads Rasmussen from Denmark performed what must be the world's longest wheelie – riding his mountain bike continuously on just one wheel for an amazing 2.3 km. As he said, 'the trick is the rider's skill and balance ability'.

Make sure your bike is correctly fitted to suit your size.

When cycling fast, your leg should be almost straight on the downstroke.

Saddle height

When you sit on your bike with one leg extended, that leg should be almost straight when your foot touches the pedal at the bottom of the downstroke. This is the position which will give you maximum power when riding. If your knees are too high or you can barely reach the pedals, your balance will be affected and your power reduced.

Frame size

Frames range from 35 cm (small) to 56 cm (extra large). Make sure you have the right size: you shouldn't lean too far over the handlebars or be cramped because the frame is too small. The length of the tube that runs from the handlebars to the saddle is important: you need to comfortably reach the handlebars with your elbows slightly bent.

saddle to handlebars

saddle to ground

top tube length

handlebars to ground

saddle to pedal

Bike frames come in different sizes. Some parts can be adjusted but others cannot.

TRUE Survivors

American Missy 'the missile' Giove was one of the early champions of downhill mountain bike racing. In her first four years of professional downhill racing, she broke her hand, smashed her kneecap and her heel, broke her wrist, pelvis, collar bone and her teeth! As one headline put it, 'She bicycles down mountains at speeds of up to 90 km/h. If she doesn't crash, she wins!'

Bike repairs

Keep your bike clean and **service** it regularly. Learn how to do simple repairs: they can make the difference between a long push home or continuing your ride. Be prepared, learn the skills and buy the repair kit before you need them.

What to carry

If you are going on a long ride, make sure you carry the following.

a set of spanners (to remove a wheel)

puncture repair kit

a set of Allen keys (for adjusting your saddle, for example)

tyre levers

spare inner tube

Mending a puncture

Keep your tyres inflated to the right pressure, check them often for stones and glass, and replace them when they look old and worn. This will reduce the number of punctures you get. This is how you mend a puncture.

1 Remove the wheel.

2 Remove the tyre using tyre levers.

3 Find the puncture in your inner tube.

4 Either use a puncture repair kit to put a rubber patch over the puncture or replace the inner tube with a new one.

5 Put the inner tube and tyre back on the wheel and put the wheel back on the bike.

6 Pump up the tyre and set off again.

If you are out on a ride when you get a puncture, you may be able to pump up the punctured tyre and cycle quickly to a place where you can make the repairs – off the road and against a fence or on some flat ground off a steep trail.

Gears and brakes

Learn how to make adjustments to your gears and brakes. Many clubs run bicycle repair workshops where you can learn the basic repair and maintenance skills you will need.

TRUE Survivors

In April 2010, 30-year-old Kevin Myatt was enjoying a day out on a bike trail in the Whakarewarewa Forest in New Zealand. He gathered speed to take some jumps but lost control and shot over the handlebars, landing on his back. In the crash his hand became impaled on his brake lever. He was taken to Rotorua hospital where the lever was successfully removed and he has since made a full recovery. He replaced the lever on his bike.

Basic skills

Once your bike is adjusted to suit your size, the challenge is to get to grips with the handling and the basic skills you need to ride it off-road. Always start on easy terrain and build up your skills to match the difficulty of the trail. Don't bite off more than you can chew!

Look well ahead

Learn to scan the path in front of you for dangers and **hazards**. The faster you go, the further ahead you need to look. Check the trail for deep puddles, potholes, large mud patches and obstacles such as rocks, tree branches – even other cyclists. If you take action early enough to avoid them you shouldn't need to brake quickly, which can lead to a skid and a fall. Try to steer as smoothly as possible.

Braking

Beginners often brake too sharply, which can lead to problems – you may even fly over the handlebars! Cover your brakes with your hands at all times, anticipate problems and slow down in good time. Learn which is your front brake and which the back. When braking to take a corner, make sure that you have stopped braking by the time you go round the bend.

Pedal power

For powerful pedalling, try to continue the motion on the upstroke as well as on the downstroke. That way you get more out of your effort than just pushing down and then relaxing. Think of the pedalling action as an almost complete circle of effort.

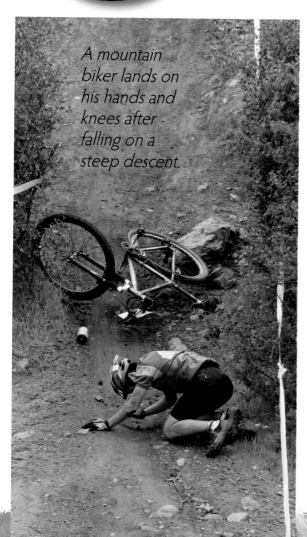

A mountain biker lands on his hands and knees after falling on a steep descent.

Using gears

Again try to look ahead and decide which gear you need to be in and change well in advance. When you see a hill coming up, change down through the gears while still on the flat. This way you won't have to grind the gears while struggling uphill.

Advanced cycling

Once you have mastered the basics, you may be ready to take on some tougher terrain. Take advice from an experienced adult and aim to progress steadily without attempting too much too soon.

Below are some techniques you need to learn to deal with steeper, longer and scarier trails. Remember to wear protective clothing while doing these.

Find your balance point

Being able to brake slowly or use a hill to bring you to a stop without putting your feet on the ground takes practice. Aim to balance your bike and yourself without falling to one side or the other. Start by facing up a gentle slope. Push forward while standing on the pedals and twist your handlebars to one side. See how long you can stay there. Try again and see whether you can do it for longer. This technique will give you confidence to stop on a track while still riding your bike. You need to master it before learning other techniques, such as hopping.

TRUE Survivors

In September 2007, Austrian racing cyclist Markus Stökl set a world record for being the fastest person on a mountain bike. He travelled to La Parva in Chile and bombed down a 1.6 km long track that was on a 45 degree slope. His maximum speed was 210.4 km/h. At that speed, one small mistake could lead to a crash that might prove fatal.

A group of riders out for an adventure on a mountain bike trail.

Steep downhill

Going steeply downhill takes skill and can be scary. You need to use your brakes all the time and control your balance. Standing up helps, shifting your weight forward and backwards to cope with the terrain. Try to keep your weight on your feet, not your arms, and stay relaxed. This helps you respond to the shape of the trail and its many bumps.

First small drop

Going over your first small step is a big moment. Try to stay relaxed as you approach. Have a plan. Will you go over one wheel at a time, landing on your front wheel? If the drop is steep on the other side, you might need to land with both tyres on the ground at the same time. If it is a bigger drop, you may even have to land rear tyre first.

This advanced rider is well protected for a steep descent in rough terrain.

23

Tricks and stunts

Experienced riders perform many amazing tricks and stunts, including the **x-up** (twisting handlebars in the air) and the **endo** (raising the rear wheel of your bike). It's best to start with some less ambitious tricks.

Rear wheel lift

Caution: with any new skill you learn, be careful when you practise, wear protective clothing and a helmet. Practise in an area with lots of space.

Front wheel lift

Cycle along slowly, and lift the front wheel a little off the ground by tightening your arms and pulling back on the handlebars. Shift your weight towards the back of the bike too. Don't be too ambitious or you might flip backwards! Once you have mastered this, you could progress to doing a wheelie.

Rear wheel lift

Ride along and then apply your brakes. At the same time, push down into the pedals and shift your weight forwards over the handlebars. Try to lift your rear wheel a couple of centimetres off the ground. Once you become more confident, you will be able to lift it higher.

Bunny hop

Amazing FACTS

The world record for a single standing bunny hop is held by Spain's Benito Ros Charral. In 2009 in Heubach, Germany, he hopped over a pole set an incredible 1.42 metres high from a standing start.

Riding steps

Bunny hops

Put an obstacle in front of your bike, such as a piece of wood, to hop your bike over. Start by lifting the front wheel over the piece of wood. Next try lifting your rear wheel over the wood. Then try lifting both wheels off together – this is the bunny hop.

Riding steps

Start with just a couple of steps and build up. Cycle slowly to the top of the steps, and let your front wheel go over. Stand on the pedals, keep relaxed and springy, and let your weight go backwards. This will help you control the second step. Once you are comfortable with two steps, try tackling a few more.

Mountain bike racing

Today there are mountain biking world championships and a world cup series. It first became an Olympic sport at the 1996 Olympics, when downhill races were held.

There are many exciting race competitions you can follow or even take part in. Here are some of them.

Mountain bike racing is the ultimate challenge for this young competitor.

Downhill racers set off at different times on a steep downhill track. The winner is the fastest person to get down the track successfully. There are many thrills and spills on the way!

over a course on which they have to do tricks and race for the finish line.

Free ride compares the skills and techniques of riders. Four riders set off

Dirt jumping also tests the skills of the riders, who have to make lots of jumps from hills of dirt high in the air, performing tricks along the way.

Competition FACTS

The youngest person to win a mountain bike world championship title was just 16. In 2001, Sam Hill from Australia came third in the championships at Vail in Colorado.

The 2011 world downhill champion is Danny Hart, from Great Britain. He sealed his success at Champery in France. Competing in pouring rain, he beat the rest of the field in an extraordinary run down a steep wooded trail to win the title.

Cross-country takes place on a trail about 8 km long over varied ground. All the racers start together and compete against each other to finish first.

Marathon racing takes place over long distances. Racers compete on a trail about 80 km long in mountainous terrain.

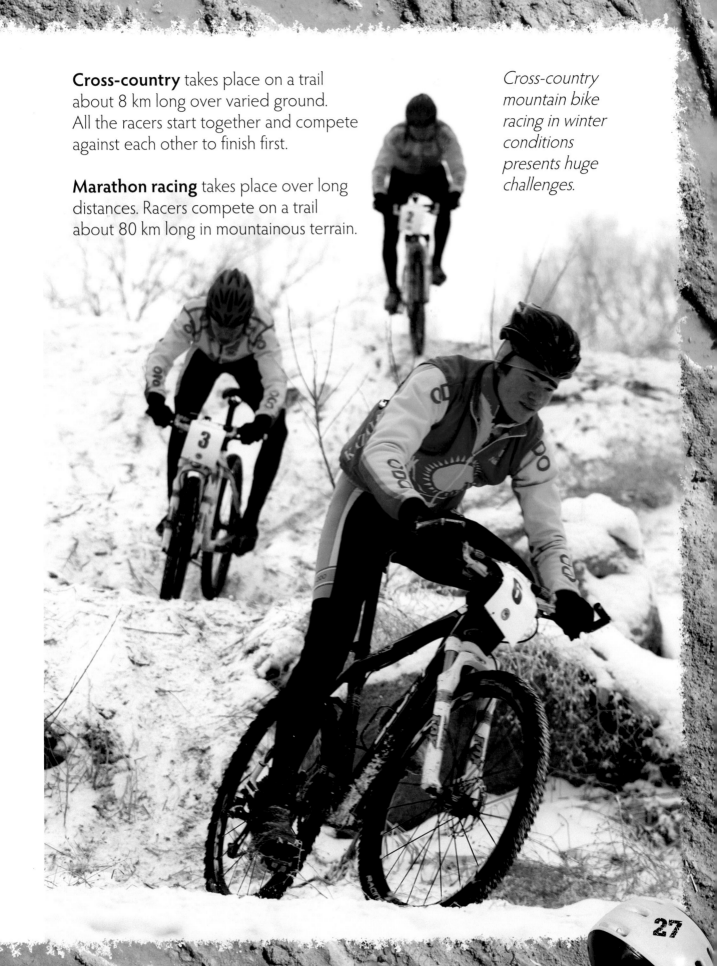

Cross-country mountain bike racing in winter conditions presents huge challenges.

What do you know about mountain biking?

Are you ready to take on the challenge of a steep mountain trail? Could you take a drop over a one metre rock, stop and balance on your bike, or anticipate danger along a trail? Try this quiz to find out just how much you know about the **adrenalin**-filled world of mountain biking. The answers are on page 31.

1 Which statement is correct?
a The longest mountain bike race runs from Canada to Mexico through the Rocky Mountains?
b The highest mountain bike races take place on Everest.
c Mountain biking started in the 1970s in California.
d You cannot start mountain biking until you are 18 years old.

2 Mountain biking is the skill of pushing your bike up mountains.
True or false?

3 The Cliffs of Moher on the west coast of Ireland are home to one of the scariest mountain bike trails on the planet.
True or false?

4 Which of these is not a hazard you would expect to find on a mountain bike trail?
a. Tree branches
b Muddy puddles
c Steep terrain
d A shark

5 Where is the Yungas Road, one of the most dangerous routes to cycle in the world?
a France **b** Bolivia **c** Hawaii **d** South Africa

6 An endo is:
a Stopping suddenly and going up on to your front tyre.
b The trick of being able to cycle backwards.
c A stunt in which you take off and land on your back wheel.
d A term your mates shout out when you cross the finishing line of a downhill race.

7 The world's strongest bike is made from
a Wood
b Titanium
c Aluminium
d Kevlar and carbon fibres

8 You don't need a helmet on a downhill mountain bike trail.
True or false?

9 When sitting on your saddle, the foot of your straightened leg should touch the pedal on its downstroke in a correctly sized bike.
True or false?

10 Which of the following don't you need in your bike repair kit?
a Tyre levers
b Puncture repair kit
c Map of the countryside
d A set of Allen keys

11 Dirt jumping is:
a What you do when you try to avoid muddy or dirty parts of a mountain bike trail.
b A type of mountain bike competition, where the riders have to perform a series of stunts taking off from dirt mounds.
c Avoiding bad comments from your friends about your style of riding.
d A training exercise to get you fit for mountain biking.

Glossary

absorb To soak up. On a mountain bike this refers to the cushioning effect a springy bike suspension has when you go over rocky ground. You feel fewer jolts and bumps than when riding a rigid bike.

adrenalin A chemical made in our bodies to help us run fast from danger or fight it.

circuit A course around a track or trail, usually finishing at the point where you started.

concussion An injury to the brain in which a violent jolt or bump can cause the brain to stop functioning properly for a short period of time. Loss of vision or memory are examples of this.

design The features on your bike (number of gears, size of tyres, suspension) that make it good for a certain type of riding and terrain.

endo An uncontrolled endo is a sudden stop which locks the front wheel, sending the back wheel up in the air, and the rider over the handlebars. In a controlled endo, the rider stops and balances on the front wheel.

frame The main structure of a bike is its frame. It is made of tubes of metal with the saddle and two wheels attached.

friction When two surfaces touch and rub against each other, friction occurs. The energy of movement is turned to heat.

hazards Anything that can cause you harm is a hazard – tree branches, skiddy mud patches, holes, steep drops and so on.

impact Impact is the force that comes from the bumpy ground you are riding on, up through the bike and into your body.

Kevlar A very strong man-made material used to make a range of things from bike tyres to body armour.

pannier A type of bag that fits on a bike. You can carry your bicycle repair kit in one.

service Giving your bike a service means checking all the main parts (such as brakes and gears), replacing any worn bits, and oiling the chain and wheel hubs.

suspension Bikes with suspension built into the front forks feel springy. The suspension helps to cushion the bumps coming up from the rough ground through the tyres.

terrain The type of landscape and ground that you ride over – a muddy forest trail or a rocky mountain track.

titanium Titanium is a very strong and light chemical which does not rust easily. These properties make it good for building bike frames.

wheelie The skill of being able to cycle along on your back wheel alone.

x-up A stunt jump done on a mountain bike, that involves turning the handlebars 180° into an 'x' shape while you fly through the air.

Websites

www.imba.org The International Mountain Bike Association
www.mbr.co.uk The Mountain Bike Rider
www.mountainbike.com USA mountain bike website
www.ambc.com.au Australian website
www.mountainbike.co.nz New Zealand website

Books

Mastering Mountain Bike Skills Brian Lopes and Lee McCormack, Human Kinetics, 2005
The Mountain Bike Book Steve Worland, Haynes Publishing, 2003
Mountain Biking: Tricks and Techniques Martyn Ashton, Cordee, 2010
Great Cycle Journeys of the World Steve Razzetti, New Holland Publishers, 2010

Quiz answers

1 *a, c*   **5** *b*   **9** *True*

2 *False*   **6** *a*   **10** *c*

3 *True*   **7** *d*   **11** *b*

4 *d*   **8** *False*

Index